Nontoxic
Housecleaning

WITHDRAWN

AMY KOLB NOYES

Chelsea Green Publishing
White River Junction, Vermont

*This book is dedicated in memory of my mom,
who taught me to care for my home,
and for my dad, who taught me to care for my planet.*

Printed in Canada
First printing, August 2009
10 9 8 7 6 5 4 3 2 1   09 10 11 12 13

DISCLAIMER: The advice in this book is believed to be correct at the time of printing, but the author and publishers accept no liability for actions inspired by this book.

Our Commitment to Green Publishing
Chelsea Green sees publishing as a tool for cultural change and ecological stewardship. We strive to align our book manufacturing practices with our editorial mission and to reduce the impact of our business enterprise in the environment. We print our books and catalogs on chlorine-free recycled paper, using vegetable-based inks whenever possible. This book may cost slightly more because we use recycled paper, and we hope you'll agree that it's worth it. Chelsea Green is a member of the Green Press Initiative (www.greenpressinitiative.org), a nonprofit coalition of publishers, manufacturers, and authors working to protect the world's endangered forests and conserve natural resources. *Nontoxic Housecleaning* was printed on Silva Enviro, a 100-percent postconsumer recycled paper supplied by Marquis.

Library of Congress Cataloging-in-Publication Data
Noyes, Amy Kolb, 1969-
  Nontoxic housecleaning / Amy Kolb Noyes.
    p. cm.
  Includes bibliographical references.
  ISBN 978-1-60358-203-2
1. House cleaning. 2. Green products. 3. Cleaning compounds. I. Title.
TX324.N693 2009
668'.1--dc22
                              2009025038

Chelsea Green Publishing Company
Post Office Box 428
White River Junction, VT 05001
(802) 295-6300
www.chelseagreen.com

CONTENTS

INTRODUCTION

Why use nontoxic cleaners? To answer that question, let's first look at why most of us don't.

Let me be perfectly clear: There is a reason why your local supermarket has an entire aisle dedicated to household cleaners. Most people, myself included, view housecleaning as a dreaded but necessary chore. This is why making cleaning your home as quick, easy, and painless as possible is big business. After all, who wants to spend all day scrubbing bathtub mildew or making the toaster shine? A cleaner that allows us to spray, wipe, and move on to other things is highly valued in our society.

But think of the price we, our children, our pets, and our planet are paying for that level of convenience. Toxic cleaners pollute our water table. They can kill wildlife when not disposed of properly. Some even pose health risks to people and pets living in your own home, especially those who do the most cleaning and breathe in the most fumes. That price is too high. Perhaps the question should be: Why *not* use nontoxic cleaners? Convenience is no longer a good enough answer.

Toxic is a relative term, and common sense should be applied to the use of all cleaning products described in this guide. If something is toxic, that means it is poisonous. With a few exceptions, such as some applications of washing soda, the ingredients recommended in this guide are safe to touch with your bare skin. Caution should also be exercised when using concentrated ingredients such as essential oils, some of which can be caustic if undiluted. Most ingredients used in the guide are, in fact, edible. That said, none of the recipes are intended for ingestion. The term *nontoxic* is used in this guide to indicate that these recipes *will not* emit poisonous fumes in your home, and they *will* break down into harmless, organic substances rather than something that will poison the natural world.

After reading this guide and trying some of its techniques and recipes I hope you'll discover, as I have, that natural homemade cleaners are inexpensive, fun to make, and satisfying to use. Many of these cleaners can be made in a large batch (one spray bottle full) and kept under the sink for future use, just like their commercial counterparts.

There is sometimes a tradeoff for giving up the toxic chemicals that make up so many commercial cleaners. In some cases, but by no means every case, your homemade cleaner might require a little extra effort to do the job. That effort might come in the form of time, heat, or muscle power. For example, it may take an hour of soaking in vinegar to remove a hard-water ring from around your bathroom drain. It may take a 200°F (93°C) oven to help clean the baked-on drips from the oven floor. And it might take a little extra elbow grease to make your good silver shine using just toothpaste—but you'll never have second thoughts about whether it's safe to put that shiny fork in your mouth!

While some dismiss homemade cleaning products as time consuming, I think you'll discover much of that extra time involves letting something soak a bit and coming back to it later. If you are a multitasker like me, that shouldn't be a problem. Like many changes, once you get used to the new routine, you'll wonder what all the fuss was about.

Other books on the topic of nontoxic and environmentally safe housekeeping spend many pages convincing the reader that toxic cleaners are bad for the home and the environment. They list harmful ingredients found in commercial products and all the reasons why they should not be used. While this is certainly enlightening, I did not feel it necessary to repeat that information here. (I have included some of the more informative books on this subject in the resources list at the back of the book.) I am working on the premise that anyone reading this guide has already chosen to clean green, and need not be convinced. Instead, I will focus on the recommended ingredients, and how and why they work.

One of the reasons I started experimenting with homemade cleaners was witnessing the dramatic effect some commercial cleaners had on my mother. She had a severe reaction to ammonia-based cleaners and had to be extremely careful about what products she used at home. Even shopping in a store that mopped the floor with ammonia would cause her to become dizzy and disoriented.

Once I started making and using natural cleaners, I immediately noticed the absence of my own reactions to commercial cleaning products: no more stinging eyes, itchy skin, or runny nose when cleaning. I also noticed the effect on my wallet. Natural cleaning ingredients, even when pricey essential oils are used, are far less expensive than commercial cleaners. And by reusing spray bottles and other containers, I could feel good about saving money and reducing waste.

Packaging

One of the things I find most satisfying about homemade cleaners is the ability to forego all the extraneous packaging that comes with commercial products, and reuse a few containers over and over again. You'll want a couple of spray bottles, which can be easily obtained by thoroughly rinsing out a used commercial spray-cleaner bottle. I've reused all sorts of bottles, from liquid hand-soap dispensers (good for dishwashing soap) to empty spice containers with shaker tops (good for dry scouring powders).

Glass canning jars work well for gooey items such as furniture polishes, be they oil or wax based. One of my favorite "dollar store" finds is a glass jar with a metal shaker top, the sort that are common in pizza restaurants containing parmesan cheese, red pepper flakes, and the like. I use mine for the nontoxic sink scrubber I use instead of bleach scrubbing cleansers. I am very careful, however, to keep the shaker clearly labeled with its contents, and I never store it in the kitchen. Although nontoxic, the cleaner is not intended for ingestion (and it would taste lousy on pizza)!

Once you start making your own cleaners, your recycling bin becomes a handy resource and not just a place to discard things. If you do find yourself experimenting with old ketchup and mustard bottles and such, just be sure to soak off any old labels and clearly mark the container with its new contents.

Cleaning from Scratch

Cleaning from scratch is a lot like cooking from scratch. In both cases it is often quicker and easier to go to the store and buy a prepared product, but that convenience comes with hidden costs. Quite often that prepared product, be it food or a cleaner, contains less than healthful ingredients, comes in too much unnecessary packaging, and is expensive. In other words, we pay for that level of convenience with our personal health and the health of our environment—as well as with our wallets.

Just as many supermarkets now offer healthier food options, more and more "natural" or "green" cleaning products can also be found in stores. Like prepared "health food," some of the products on the market are just as safe and are of similar quality to what you could make at home. Usually, however, you will pay a stiff premium for what would cost far less if you made it from scratch. And once you learn just how easy it is to make these cleaners, you'll be glad to keep that premium for yourself.

When cooking from scratch, you have the advantage of preparing foods just the way you like them. If you're more partial to lime than lemon, you can swap lime juice for lemon juice in your tabouli salad. Likewise, if you prefer the scent of lavender over pine, you can scent your kitchen spray cleanser with lavender essential oil instead of pine. Much like cooking, there is room for creativity and customization.

That said, it should also be noted that both cooking and creating cleaning products involve a little basic chemistry. The better you understand that chemistry, the more successful you will be at creating your own recipes.

The Chemistry

Different cleaners work in different ways. Kitchen-appliance cleaners need to dissolve grease and kill bacteria. A bathroom cleaner should kill germs and take care of "soap scum" and any other deposits left behind by hard water. Furniture polish must treat wood as well as pick up dust. Floor cleaners have to both break down and pick up all sorts of dirt. The chemical properties of the various cleaners allow them to take on specific tasks.

It takes an acidic substance, like vinegar, to unlock an alkaline (basic) stain such as hard-water mineral deposits. It takes a basic substance, such as baking soda, to neutralize acid-based odors. Furthermore, it takes an abrasive substance, such as salt crystals, to coax up tough stains such as baked-on drips in the oven. And it takes a substance with disinfecting properties to kill germs and mold.

Disinfectants kill bacteria and molds (but not necessarily their spores or viruses). In the United States, the Environmental Protection Agency (EPA) has strict standards as to what can be labeled a disinfectant. Disinfectants must have at least a 99 percent kill rate and be registered with the EPA as a pesticide. The white vinegar you can buy by the gallon at the supermarket nearly reaches that benchmark, but cannot claim to be a disinfectant as defined by the EPA. Likewise, borax kills microorganisms but is not officially listed as a disinfectant. Sunshine is one of the best natural disinfectants, killing bacteria and molds—best of all it's free!

There are also many antibacterial herbs and essential oils that have been used for centuries, including rosemary, spearmint, ginger, and orange. Some of the best oils for homemade cleaners also have antifungal and antiviral, as well as antibacterial properties. Among these are tea tree oil, eucalyptus, lavender, lemon, and thyme.

Part 1

THE BASIC TOOLBOX

Most of the basic ingredients you'll need to make your own household cleaners can be found at your supermarket, although not all of them will be in the cleaning aisle. A few ingredients may require a special trip to a co-op or health food store, if your local supermarket does not have a sizable "natural foods" section. Many of these items may already be in your cupboard.

The Big Three:

- Baking soda (the little yellow box you keep in the refrigerator)
- White vinegar, 5 percent acidity (this is your normal, everyday plain vinegar)
- Soap (or detergent, if hard water is a concern)

Baking Soda

That little yellow box absorbing odors in your refrigerator and/or freezer is also a star of natural cleaners. Sodium bicarbonate, a.k.a. baking soda, is a mineral derived from soda ash. It is slightly alkaline and neutralizes acidic things, such as odors in liquids caused by acids, so it works on laundry, in drains and garbage disposals, and even on tough problems such as pet urine. Baking soda's abrasive texture makes it ideal for scrubbing surfaces such as sinks, counters, appliances, and bathroom fixtures. If you adopt no other techniques in this book, you will still be making a big difference by swapping your toxic scouring powder for plain baking soda.

Vinegar

Distilled 5 percent white vinegar can be purchased economically in gallon jugs at many supermarkets. When a recipe in this book calls for vinegar, it always refers to distilled 5 percent white vinegar. Other vinegars, such as apple cider and red wine vinegar, can leave behind stains—not what you want in a household cleaner. Vinegar, for cleaning purposes, is the opposite of baking soda. It is acidic and thus neutralizes alkaline substances. Like all acids, vinegar corrodes and dissolves. For example, it will break down "hard-water" mineral buildup on sinks and tubs. It also dissolves tarnish from metals such as brass and copper.

Vinegar is a powerful sanitizer. Although it is not officially recognized by the EPA as a disinfectant, it is commonly known to kill bacteria, molds, and other microbes. While the smell of vinegar can be overwhelming, it dissipates after a couple of hours.

Liquid Soap or Detergent

Unless I specify otherwise, whenever I refer to soap in this guide I mean a liquid soap. Purists insist upon using castile soap, which has a vegetable- or nut-oil base. Other soaps use an animal product, such as beef tallow, as their necessary fat. (Soap is formed through a process called saponification, in which fats chemically react with a strong alkali, such as lye.) Detergents work like soaps, but are made from synthetic ingredients. Detergents were developed during World War II, when the oils used to make soap were scarce. They are generally made from petroleum products with added surfactants and foaming agents.

That said, there are some very good phosphate-free, biodegradable detergents on the market that are free of artificial dyes and perfumes, and are not tested on animals. (Phosphates are a problem because, as they build up, they pollute waterways and can cause fish kills and other ecological damage.) The major advantage of a detergent is that it does not react, as soap does, to minerals in hard water. The evidence of this reaction is commonly referred to as "soap scum" that can build up on shower walls and cause white laundry to dull and turn gray. Those with soft water need not worry much about such reactions.

I personally prefer to use a castile soap that has been scented with an essential oil such as peppermint, sweet orange, or lavender. This reduces the amount of essential oil I add to my homemade cleansers, thus keeping down the end cost. Dr. Bronner's is a widely available brand that is made with organic oils, is certified fair trade, is not tested on animals, and is available already scented with essential oil. Vermont Soap Organics is another popular brand.

These three ingredients will take you far. When combined in a cleaner, a castile soap scented with an essential oil will mask some of the vinegar scent. Additional oils can be added to customize your cleaner and to boost certain cleaning properties. For example, just a few drops of tea tree oil will help combat bathroom mold and mildew.

Note that vinegar's scent will dissipate fairly quickly. While it may smell strong at first, it will not linger as the scents of some synthetic cleaners are meant to do. Therefore, it only takes a few drops of essential oil to scent a whole bottle of homemade spray cleaner. As the smell of vinegar fades it is the essential oil that will leave a lasting impression.

Other Key Ingredients:

While the big three listed above are a good place to start, there are several other ingredients that will go a long way in helping to safely clean your home. A few ingredients, including essential oils, can be pricey. However, these are used in minute quantities and a little bottle goes a long way!

Borax

Borax is often found at the supermarket with the laundry products. A popular brand is 20 Mule Team borax, sold by the Dial Corporation as a "natural laundry booster and multi-purpose household cleaner." Borax is a powdered form of a naturally occurring mineral composed of sodium, boron, oxygen, and water. It is not harmful to washing machines, plumbing, or septic tanks and does not contain phosphates or chlorine. My grandmother first introduced me to borax when my daughter was born and I was looking for something to soak cloth diapers in between laundry loads. I soon discovered borax has uses beyond the laundry, in virtually every room of the house as a nonabrasive cleanser, deodorizer, and stain remover. It will make porcelain enamel bathroom surfaces shine and it can clean hand-painted china without scratching or fading.

Washing Soda

Washing soda (sodium carbonate) is like baking soda on steroids. It is much more alkaline, and thus caustic. The manufacturer warns that you should wear rubber gloves when using washing soda "in a solution or paste," as is often the case in the recipes herein. For this reason, I prefer baking soda for everyday cleaning. I reserve my washing soda for really tough and/or smelly cleaning problems.

Among washing soda's virtues is its ability to tackle grease as well as run-of-the-mill dirt. It is marketed as a laundry booster as it effectively combats hard water and its resulting dingy laundry. Washing soda also shares baking soda's ability to neutralize odors.

Arm & Hammer sells washing soda under the name Super Washing Soda. While the manufacturer lists a number of cleaning tasks it can tackle (from pots and pans to concrete garage floors), there are a few uses it cautions against. These include aluminum surfaces, no-wax floors, and fiberglass sinks and tubs, which washing soda will scratch.

Lemon Juice

For those of you who just can't put up with the smell of vinegar, lemon juice is a viable alternative for cleaning jobs requiring an acid, such as hard-water stains, tarnish, dissolving waxy buildup, and cleaning wood. Lemon juice in your laundry's rinse water will also serve as a mild bleach for clothes that are hung out to dry in the sun.

Water

All right, this may seem obvious but is worth repeating here: The combination of soap and water kills germs and cleans away dirt. Water is also used to dilute spray-cleaning formulas so they can be easily applied with a reusable spray bottle. Some recipes call for hot water, others cold. Most recipes are not temperature dependent.

Club Soda

Your grandmother was right: Club soda is great for getting out stains—and not only for emergency laundry mishaps. Club soda works on carpet and upholstery stains as well.

Cooking Oils

Olive oil, nut oils, and plain old vegetable oil all play a part in nontoxic cleaning—especially when it comes to conditioning natural materials such and wood and leather. For cleaning purposes it would be a shame to use extra virgin or virgin olive oil. They're far more expensive, and no more suitable, than lower grades labeled as "pure olive oil" or "olive oil."

Linseed/Flaxseed Oil

Food-grade linseed oil, also known as flaxseed or omega-3 oil, is a main ingredient in both floor-wax recipes provided in this guide. The food-grade oil differs from the product sold by the gallon at hardware stores, which contains toxic additives. If available, choose boiled food-grade linseed oil since it has a faster drying time than raw linseed oil.

Essential Oils

Essential oils are a natural way to scent your homemade cleaning solutions. Some, such as clove, lavender, rosemary, lemon, orange, and tea tree oils, are also natural antiseptics. Tea tree oil is perhaps the most effective essential oil for a multipurpose cleanser as it is known to be quite effective at killing mold. That said, tea tree oil's strong scent is a turnoff for some people. Mixing in a few drops of your favorite mint, citrus, or floral oil will help take the edge off.

Grapefruit-Seed Extract

This is another excellent mold killer, and does not come with a strong smell as does its natural counterparts, tea tree oil and vinegar. Its major downsides are price and availability. Once you have located

a source, a little goes a long way. About 20 drops can be diluted in a quart of water and still be effective.

Bar Soap

Castile soap comes in bar form, but can be difficult to find outside health food stores. Ivory Soap, with its nearly neutral pH and lack of added dyes and/or moisturizers, is a readily available alternative. Bar soap makes for an excellent laundry stain stick. No matter the brand, just be sure there is no added coloring, moisturizers, or heavy perfume.

Salt

Salt is a key ingredient in a few nontoxic cleaning remedies, including the solutions for some tough problems like clogged drains and oven spills. Because it is abrasive, salt is also good for scrubbing up tough stains.

Wheat Bran

Wheat bran is both abrasive and absorbent, and therefore is an effective stain fighter. It can be used on carpets, rugs, and most fabrics. Unprocessed bran can be found in the supermarket cereal aisle.

Glycerin

Vegetable glycerin, available at heath food stores, is a good standby for tough stains on hard surfaces such as countertops and appliances. A thin application on the bathroom mirror will also keep it from fogging during your shower.

Beeswax

Beeswax is a natural wax produced by bees, with many household uses—from floor wax to all-natural scented candles.

Cornstarch

Cornstarch is a fabulously diverse cleaning ingredient. Dry cornstarch can be used to absorb carpet stains or made into a paste with water to clean windows. Dilute it further to serve as a spray starch for laundry. You can even put it in your mop water to clean linoleum floors.

Cream of Tartar

A byproduct of winemaking, cream of tartar is often used in baking and can be found along with the spices and baking supplies in your local supermarket. As a cleaner, cream of tartar can combat hard-water stains on porcelain sinks and tubs. It's also useful for scrubbing brass or copper cookware.

Hydrogen Peroxide

Hydrogen peroxide is commonly sold in a solution diluted to 3 percent. It can be found in the drugstore in a brown bottle (it breaks down when exposed to light). A stronger solution of hydrogen peroxide is also on the market, but 3 percent is strong enough for everyday cleaning uses. At that concentration, hydrogen peroxide is an environmentally friendly bleach that kills molds and bacteria.

Tools of the Trade

All of the recipes in this guide can be mixed up and stored in either a glass jar or a reusable plastic spray bottle. Please be sure to clearly label all containers for safety's sake and to avoid future confusion. Like commercial cleaning products, homemade products should be kept out of the reach of children and pets.

In general, sponges and cotton cloths make great applicators and scrubbers. You'll also want something more abrasive, such as a scrub brush or scouring pad, for those jobs that require a little more muscle power. Remember, while natural cleaners can measure up to their synthetic counterparts, sometimes a little more scrubbing or a little longer soaking is required.

Sponges

All sponges are not created equal. Some sponges are injected with poisonous ingredients to keep them from smelling musty. Seek out a plain cellulose sponge that does not make any antimicrobial claims. A better way to keep your sponge or dishcloth from getting musty is to microwave it for a minute or so after use, thus killing any microorganisms it may have picked up. You can also clean sponges in a dishwashing machine, along with the dishes.

The eraser-style sponges that are relatively new to the market are a great nontoxic cleaning tool. These sponges work by virtue of their micro-abrasive texture to seemingly erase dirt, grease, and even crayon from walls, counters, appliances, and other surfaces. Owing to their abrasiveness, eraser-style sponges are not recommended for surfaces that may scratch or dull, such as some metal finishes or glossy surfaces—see product packaging for precise recommendations. Eraser sponges can be used with just water or in conjunction with one of the multipurpose cleaners described in this guide.

Scrubbers

There's nothing like a copper scrubber to make pots and pans shine. These scrubbers work best on copper, stainless steel, and cast iron cookware and tough scrubbing jobs like stove burners, oven racks, and barbecue grills. Unlike steel wool, they won't rust or splinter from use. They should not be used on surfaces prone to scratching, such as cookware with nonstick coatings. It's worth noting that nonstick coatings themselves can emit toxins, especially when used at very high temperatures. If you are striving for a nontoxic home, you're better off with traditional nonstick cookware, like a properly seasoned cast iron skillet.

Scrub Brushes

A good scrub brush is a must for tough jobs like very dirty floors and carpet stains. For small areas, such as sink drains and small stains, an old toothbrush does the trick.

Dust Cloths

Microfiber dust cloths, sold under several brand names, are great at trapping dust without the need for special sprays. These work well for everyday dusting and sweeping up hard-surface floors. They can be shaken out and reused several times, and are as good as new after being run through the laundry. Microfiber cloths should be used dry. However, when dusting with a regular dust cloth, always dampen the cloth to keep dust from flying away and resettling.

Towels and Rags

Paper or cloth? I prefer cotton kitchen towels and dish rags to paper towels. Cloth is tougher, better for scrubbing, equally or more absorbent, and can be washed and reused again and again. That said, there are instances when the convenience of a paper towel can't be denied. I look for paper towels made from recycled paper and without chlorine bleach. As some consolation for being disposable, these can be composted instead of thrown away as trash. I also prefer "select-a-size" towels, which allow me to use only a small piece when that's all that's needed.

Vacuum Cleaner/Sweeper

Don't underestimate the value of a good vacuum! I use a vacuum with a HEPA filter (High Efficiency Particulate Air filter) that traps allergens, preventing them from reentering the room. I nearly always reach for the vacuum or my push-powered sweeper when cleaning hard-surface floors. Brooms have a tendency to scatter dust into the air, only to have it resettle moments later. Vacuums and sweepers capture the dirt and keep it from recirculating. For those who prefer to conserve energy even in cleaning, a nonelectric sweeper is the tool of choice. As for vacuums, they aren't just for floors. I use all my vacuum attachments to take care of cleaning upholstered furniture and even dusting bookshelves and lampshades.

Dust Mop

I use my dust mop to shine up my wood floors. Microfiber dust mops can be used dry, but traditional dust mops need to be lightly dampened to hold onto the dust. Try mixing up a batch of one of the floor cleaner recipes from this guide in a spray bottle. This can be kept on hand for spraying the bottom of the mop before you dust.

Looking to put a shine on that wood floor? Reach for a homemade floor polish, or even a furniture polish to spray on the mop; just beware that oils will make the floor slippery until they are fully absorbed.

Pantyhose

Don't throw out pantyhose with runs; move them out of your dresser and into the pantry with the cleaning supplies. Pantyhose make great sink scrubbers by rolling them in a ball, tying them in a knot, or stuffing the toe with a bar of soap.

Spray Bottles

Spray bottles come in many sizes. The best spray bottle to use is one you've rescued from the recycle bin. Most recipes herein are customized to common 32-ounce (large) and 16-ounce (small) bottles. Obviously, recipes can be doubled or halved to suit your container.

Part 2

ROOM BY ROOM

Kitchen

Of all the rooms in your home, it is likely the kitchen you most often find yourself cleaning. In addition to cooking and eating areas, the kitchen is often home to messy projects. It can also be the social hub of a home, and thus an area you want to look good all the time.

Multi-surface sprays that can take care of countertops as well as glass oven windows are popular for their ease and convenience. You can make your own by mixing 1 cup of vinegar and 1 Tablespoon of lemon juice with 3 cups of water in a large spray bottle. Just shake, spray on, wipe off, and you're finished!

In kitchens, we need to worry about disinfecting as well as cleaning. For this reason a spray bottle filled with $2/3$ cup of vinegar and 1 Tablespoon of soap, diluted in 1 cup of warm water, makes an excellent all-purpose kitchen cleaner. A squeeze of lemon juice is a nice addition to help cut grease and make the mixture smell better. The smell of vinegar dissipates within a couple of hours, and the lemon helps mask the smell in the meantime. Alternatively, a few drops of essential oil such as lavender will do the trick. To keep the soap from clumping, dilute it in warm water before adding the vinegar and lemon juice.

Countertops and Cutting Boards

The all-purpose cleaners described above work great for wiping off counters and cutting boards. For an extra punch, sprinkle baking soda directly onto the cutting surface and wipe clean with a damp sponge. The baking soda will absorb cutting-board odors and act as an abrasive to help get up tough spills. Rubbing the cutting board with a lemon wedge is another great way to keep it clean and smelling fresh.

Keeping straight vinegar in a kitchen spray bottle is another good way to disinfect. Make spraying your cutting surfaces the last thing you do before turning the kitchen lights out for the night. There's no need to rinse, and the vinegar smell will be long gone by morning. Vinegar will also kill kitchen molds if used in this manner around the sink or other wet areas.

A spray bottle of 3 percent hydrogen peroxide will also disinfect cutting surfaces, killing bacteria such as salmonella. Simply spray countertops and cutting surfaces. Let sit for a few minutes, then wipe with a dry kitchen towel. If using hydrogen peroxide in a spray bottle be sure the bottle is properly labeled and is not translucent, as the hydrogen peroxide breaks down if exposed to light. Be aware that hydrogen peroxide is a bleach, so wipe dry with a white towel or a towel you don't mind lightening.

Fruits and Vegetables

The hydrogen peroxide spray above also serves as a great bacteria-killing fruit and veggie wash. Just spray on and rinse under cold water.

Another good fruit and vegetable wash is a Tablespoon of vinegar diluted in 6 cups of cold water. Put the vinegar and water in a large bowl or pot and soak the fruits and vegetables for about a minute. Rinse thoroughly.

Drains

Drains harbor germs, so it's important to disinfect them regularly. It's a good idea to pour ½ cup of straight white vinegar down the drain a couple of times a week. Another simple way to give your drain some regular maintenance, perhaps once a month, is to mix ¼ to ½ cup of vinegar with an equal amount of baking soda in the sink with the drain open. Flush with a kettle-full of boiling water after a half-hour or so.

If you have a clogged drain, use a plunger, wire coat hanger, or snake to clear the clog. Then pour ½ cup of salt and ½ cup of baking soda down the drain, followed by 1 to 2 quarts of boiling water. Let the sink sit unused overnight, then flush with cold water the next day.

Clogs can also be treated with borax. Pour ¼ cup down the drain and let sit for ten minutes. Flush with boiling water, poured in a little at a time as it drains. This technique may need to be repeated.

Dishes

A plain castile soap, or any phosphate-free soap, is recommended for hand dishwashing. A few drops of an essential oil (such as clove, lavender, rosemary, lemon, orange, or tea tree oil) can be mixed as an added disinfectant.

Automatic Dishwashing

Automatic dishwashers are designed to be used with commercial dishwasher detergents, and I haven't found a reliable alternative that

is effective under regular use. Instead, I purchase a phosphate-free dishwasher detergent, which is better for the earth's waterways by not introducing phosphates into the water table.

That said, the following formula works to clean an occasional load of dishes. However, it tends to leave a film on dishes, especially glassware. When I have run out of dishwasher detergent and don't want to make a special trip to the store, I fill the dishwasher's soap dispenser with a mix of equal parts washing soda and borax (my machine takes ¼ cup each when filling both the prewash and wash dispensers). Then, at the beginning of the dishwasher's rinse cycle, I open the door and toss in a couple of Tablespoons of white vinegar to aid in rinsing off any film the borax and washing soda have left behind.

Glassware/Crystal

Add ¼ cup of vinegar and ¼ cup of salt to the dishwater to make glassware and crystal shine.

China

When washing fine china, add ½ cup of borax to the rinse water to give the dishes an added shine.

Porcelain

Clean porcelain items in baking soda and warm water. Use cream of tartar to remove any stains.

Pots and Pans

For a stubborn cooked-on mess at the bottom of a pot or pan, sprinkle baking soda on the problem area and cover with a half inch of water. Put the pan on the stovetop and bring to a simmer to lift off the cooked-on food.

To remove rust from old pots and pans, cut a potato in half and dip the cut surface in baking soda. Rub the banking-soda-covered potato on the rust spot, using a circular motion. Rinse and repeat until the rust is gone.

Silverware

When it comes time to polish the good silver, there are a few options. First, plain white toothpaste is a great way to make your silverware sparkle. Use a cloth to rub the toothpaste into tarnished silver; dip in warm, soapy water; rinse in warm water and buff dry.

An alternative silver polish can be fashioned from baking soda and water. Mix a few Tablespoons of baking soda with enough water to form a paste. Rub this paste onto the silver and rinse thoroughly. Or try rubbing silverware with wheat bran and vinegar, mixed to a paste consistency. Wipe off and shine with a clean cotton cloth.

The best way to prevent silver from tarnishing in the first place is to keep it in a sealed plastic bag until it needs to be used, as tarnish results from silver reacting with oxygen in the air.

Chrome Appliances

The baking soda and water mixture described above also works great on chrome. Again, apply the paste with a cloth and rinse. Alternatively, toothpaste is a wonderful chrome polish—just rub on and buff off.

Stainless Steel

Stainless-steel sinks and appliances will shine with this two-part cleaning technique. First wipe the metal with olive oil on a dishcloth, then follow by wiping with a cloth soaked in vinegar. Allow to air dry.

Brass and Copper

Cleaner

Use cream of tartar as a cleaner for brass or copper cookware.

Polish

Brass and copper items can be polished with a paste made from flour, salt, and vinegar. Add 1 teaspoon of salt and enough flour to make a paste (about 1 cup) to 1 cup of vinegar. Rub on and let sit for a half hour to an hour before rinsing. Buff with a cotton cloth moistened with vegetable oil.

Refrigerators

Clean and deodorize the fridge, inside and out, by mixing 1 Tablespoon of borax with 4 cups of warm water. Apply with a sponge and rinse with a sponge dipped in cold water.

Ovens

Let's face it. No one looks forward to having to clean the oven. It is a dreaded job, but can be made much easier if you can let the cleaning solution stay on overnight. Start by sprinkling water directly onto the

bottom of the oven. Next, cover the surface with baking soda and sprinkle a little more water on top. Let this sit overnight. In the morning wipe the mixture up with a sponge or abrasive pad. Once the water and baking soda are removed, add a few drops of liquid soap to the sponge and go over the entire oven.

If you're dealing with a lot of baked-on stains, try sprinkling baking soda on the bottom of the oven and spray on straight vinegar in a spray bottle. Scrub with a sponge as it fizzes. To do the sides and top of the oven, spray with vinegar then wipe with baking soda on a damp sponge. Use a sponge with a green scrubbie on one side so you can flip it over and scrub the tough spots. Rinse with water and a sponge. Place a mirror on the oven floor to help see what you're cleaning on the ceiling.

To keep the oven neater between cleanings, tackle spills by covering them with salt immediately after you turn the oven off, while it is still warm. When the oven cools, scrape off the salted spill (a spatula works well for this) and wipe clean with a sponge.

Stovetops

Remove burner grates and soak in a sink full of water with ½ cup of baking soda to dissolve grease. For cooked-on stains use washing soda instead of baking soda. Rinse before replacing on stove. Use baking soda on a damp sponge to wipe down the stovetop. Again, substitute washing soda when dealing with crusty cooked-on stains. (A reminder: Wear rubber gloves to prevent washing soda from being in contact with your skin.)

Kitchen Tiles

Kitchen tiles, be they on counters, floors, or backsplashes, are easily cleaned with a mixture of equal parts vinegar and hot water. This mixture need not be rinsed, but should be wiped off with a cloth. The vinegar will tackle any mold that settles in the grout. For tougher mold problems, check out the mold-killing spray recipes in the bathroom section of this guide.

A 50/50 mixture of lemon juice and water will also do the trick for kitchen tiles, as will an application of 3 percent hydrogen peroxide. Both lemon juice and hydrogen peroxide will act as a mild bleach on grout.

No-Wax Floors

No-wax floors, commonly installed in kitchens, can be vacuumed with a hard-floor vacuum head (without a beater brush) or with a nonelectric sweeper. To wash the floor, pour ¼ cup of lemon juice and no more than ¼ cup of soap into a pail with two gallons of hot water. Rinsing is not necessary, however, linoleum floors will shine when rinsed with water and a splash of skim milk.

Kitchen floors are made from all sorts of materials these days. Here's a good cleaner for pretty much any type of kitchen floor; it leaves a fresh citrus scent and a sparking clean floor:

Fabulous No-Rinse Floor Cleaner

In a bucket, mix:
> 1 gallon water
> 1 cup vinegar
> 1/3 cup castile soap (with sweet orange oil is particularly nice in this recipe)
> 2 Tablespoons lemon juice

No-Soap, No-Rinse Floor Cleaner

Vinegar works well on grungy floors, even without soap. Dilute a cup of vinegar in a bucket of water for a soap-free floor cleaner. Add a few drops of lavender and rosemary oil for a lasting, pleasant scent. Tackle any tough scuff marks with baking soda on a sponge before mopping the entire floor.

Floor Waxes

Beeswax Is Best

For floors that do require waxing, you can make your own high-quality, all-natural floor wax with the aid of a double boiler. Place the double boiler on the stovetop, with water in the bottom, and bring to a boil. Place 1 cup of food-grade linseed oil and 1 ounce of beeswax (about the same as a cube 1 inch on each side) in the top of the double boiler and stir slowly until the wax is melted and the ingredients come together. Pour this mixture into a container that can take the heat and apply to the floor with a rag. Leftovers of this recipe don't store well, so don't make more than you need at one time.

Waxless Floor Wax

Technically this is not a wax, but it will protect floors like a wax. It is easier to prepare and apply than the beeswax recipe above. The downside is it needs time to dry, then must be buffed. The measurements given are enough for a small room, but the recipe is easily doubled.

In a shallow bowl or container mix ½ cup of food-grade linseed oil and ¼ cup of lemon juice. Apply evenly to the floor with a rag. Buff smooth once dry.

Appliances/Countertops

Remove tough stains by wiping with a sponge dabbed with glycerin. Work the stain in a circular motion from the edge inward. Sprinkle baking soda over the glycerin, then wipe with a vinegar-soaked sponge.

Microwave

In a microwavable bowl mix 1 part vinegar and 2 parts water. Cook on high, uncovered, until the mixture comes to a boil. Boil solution for up to one minute. Do not allow the mixture to boil over. Do not remove bowl immediately, as liquids can become "superheated" in the microwave and boil over belatedly. With a sponge or cloth, wipe the condensation from the walls, ceiling, and floor of the microwave and the dirt will come off with it!

The above technique can also be used with 1 cup of water, 1 Tablespoon of lemon juice, and 2 Tablespoons of baking soda.

Microwave Tip: To get rid of microwave smells, place a few lemon wedges in a bowl of water and microwave on high for a couple of minutes. Once the timer goes off, leave the bowl in the microwave for a few more minutes as the water continues to let off steam. Wipe away any condensation.

Coffee Maker

Clean the inner workings of your coffee maker by running straight vinegar through a couple of cycles. If you use a reusable filter you can leave it in place (so long as it is free of coffee grounds). Simply fill the water reservoir with white vinegar and turn the machine on. Once the cycle is finished, pour the hot vinegar from the carafe back into the water reservoir and run it through again. Dump the vinegar out after two cycles through the machine. Next, fill the reservoir with water and run the water through to rinse the machine. Dump the hot water when finished and start again with fresh water. I run three rinse cycles, each with fresh water, to be sure all the vinegar is removed from the system. I know from experience that vinegar is not a good addition to your morning coffee!

Garbage Odors

Deodorize the kitchen trashcan by sprinkling either borax or baking soda on the bottom of the barrel.

Bathroom

The supermarket cleaning aisle is full of products to make your bathroom sparkle, but from bathtub mildew to toilet-bowl stains, there's not a bathroom cleaning job that can't be accomplished with natural cleaners you make yourself. The nontoxic arsenal includes disinfecting spray cleaners, gentle scrubbing cleansers, mildew killers, toilet-bowl cleaners, glass-cleaning sprays, and floor washes. What's more, you don't need to worry about ventilating harsh chemicals out of the room during and after cleaning time.

Scouring Powder

Scouring powders are abrasive cleansers that conquer soap scum, hard-water marks, and mildew by scraping them off the surface of your fixtures. Natural scouring powders are comprised of mildly abrasive minerals that should not scratch tubs and sinks. Different minerals also lend different cleaning properties. Baking soda absorbs odors, borax disinfects and kills mold, washing soda cuts greasy stains, and salt is extra abrasive. With scouring powders, the more you use the better it works—but more effort is needed to rinse it away. Therefore, use your best judgment as to how much is needed to get the job done.

Dry scouring-powder formulas can be mixed ahead of time and stored in well-marked containers. I like to mix scouring powders in reusable shaker jars, however, it is important to clearly label reused food containers. I have a glass shaker with a metal top, like those used for parmesan cheese and pepper flakes at many pizza shops. I picked it up at a dollar store and have certainly gotten my money's worth. Smaller batches can be stored in empty spice containers with shaker tops.

Salty Scouring Scrub

Add the abrasive scouring power of salt to help vinegar tackle mildew. Sprinkle salt on the problem area, then scrub with a sponge or scouring pad soaked in vinegar.

Borax Scourer

Borax is great at killing mold and mildew. If the problem area is still damp, sprinkle on borax and let it sit at least fifteen minutes before wiping it away with a damp sponge. Rinse with warm water. If the area is dry, wipe it down with a damp sponge before applying the borax. This works great on sinks and tubs, and can also be used on fiberglass surfaces without the fear of scratching. For very moldy areas, let sit overnight.

Grease-Away Scouring Powder

In a shaker container mix 3 parts baking soda to 1 part washing soda. Rub with a damp sponge. Rinse thoroughly. Washing soda should not be used on fiberglass surfaces.

Soft Scrubs

When making soft scrubs, only produce the amount needed at that time. It is easier to make soft scrubs up as needed than to store them in such a manner so that they maintain a good consistency. When making soft scrubs, mix the ingredients to a creamy texture in a small bowl and apply with a damp sponge.

Basic Soft Scrub

In a bowl mix $\frac{1}{8}$ to $\frac{1}{3}$ cup of baking soda, depending on the size of your job. Moisten with a teaspoon of liquid castile soap and stir, adding drops of soap until a creamy texture is achieved. Scoop up cleanser with a damp sponge. Clean area with sponge and rinse well.

Disinfecting Soft Scrub

Follow the directions above for basic soft scrub, replacing half the baking soda with borax.

Grime-Fighting Soft Scrub

Follow the directions for basic soft scrub, substituting washing soda for the baking soda. Be sure to wear gloves when working with washing soda and rinse the area thoroughly. Do not use on fiberglass surfaces, as it my scratch.

Mold and Mildew Killers

Mold and mildew can lurk on shower curtains, in rugs, around leaks, and between tiles. When faced with mold and mildew, most people turn to chlorine bleach. Environmentally speaking, that's a pretty drastic move. Chlorine is a lot nastier than most people realize. Try one of the following instead.

Tea Tree Sanitizer

Tea tree oil has a strong but not unpleasant smell that takes a few days to dissipate. (The same might be said for chlorine bleach.) Tea tree oil's other major drawback is that it can be expensive, but a little goes a long way. This recipe can be made in advance and kept on hand until needed. Simply mix:

> 2 teaspoons tea tree oil
> 2 cups water

Combine the above in a spray bottle, shake to blend before each use, and spray on problem areas. There is no need to rinse.

Borax-Vinegar Mix

This mixture is also best made in a spray bottle, but does not have the extended shelf life of the tea tree formula described above.

> 1 teaspoon borax
> 3 Tablespoons vinegar
> 2 cups hot water

Combine in spray bottle and shake to mix.

Spray on problem surfaces and let sit for at least five minutes before scrubbing and rinsing.

Minty Tub Scrub

For extra cleaning power, add some soap to the mix. In a spray bottle combine in the given order:

> 1 teaspoon borax
> 1 Tablespoon castile soap with peppermint oil
> 10 drops spearmint oil

1½ cups warm water
¼ cup vinegar

Shake well prior to each use.

Vinegar Spray

Five percent white distilled vinegar (the strength sold in bulk at the supermarket) reportedly kills 82 percent of molds. Pour it straight into a spray bottle, spray on the moldy area, and let set without rinsing. Then leave the room; the smell will be gone in a few hours.

Citrus-Seed-Extract Attack

Don't like strong smells? Attack mold with this odorless alternative:

20 drops citrus-seed extract
2 cups water

Combine the citrus-seed extract and water in a spray bottle, shake to blend, and apply to moldy areas. There is no need to rinse and, like the tea tree sanitizer, this mix can be stored away for later use.

Shower-Curtain Solution

Cloth shower curtains are better for you and the environment than their PVC counterparts. Shower curtains made from PVC (polyvinyl chloride) contain volatile organic compounds that give off toxic fumes, especially when the product is new. For routine cleaning, cloth shower curtains can be run through the clothes washer. To take care of a mildewy shower curtain, whether cloth or PVC, wash it in the bathtub with warm water and a cup of baking soda. Rinse well then rub with half a lemon, squeezing to release extra juice on the problem areas. Hang outside to dry in the sun.

Grout Stains Gone

You can literally erase stains from your grout with a pencil eraser. This also works on hard-water stains on bathtub caulking. Simply rub the eraser on the stains. When you're finished, vacuum up what the eraser left behind.

Sink

To clean hard-water stains and scale from the sink, sprinkle baking soda over the sink then wipe down with a vinegar-soaked sponge. For tough sink stains use an eraser-style sponge.

Hard-water stains in a porcelain sink or tub can be scrubbed with cream of tartar sprinkled on a damp sponge. For really tough stains, try applying 3 percent hydrogen peroxide to the scale. Let soak a few minutes before wiping away.

To clean the drain ring, put a dab of toothpaste on an old toothbrush and brush in a circular motion, paying special attention to the groove around the ring.

For stubborn hard-water scale, soak a cloth in vinegar and let it sit on the stain for an hour or more. Wipe with the cloth when finished. Lemon juice can be used in the same fashion as vinegar to combat drain scale.

Bath

Cut soap scum without scratching bathtub fixtures and surfaces by scrubbing surfaces with a balled-up pair of old pantyhose. Use with

one of the scouring powder, soft scrub, or spray-cleaner formulas listed in this section, and say goodbye to that ring around the tub!

Tackling the Toilet Bowl

Toilet bowls are natural havens for odors and germs. Fortunately, there are some simple ways to take care of these problems. The following recipes range from light everyday deodorizers to deep cleansers. They are all used in conjunction with a good swish and scrub with a toilet brush.

Bright-Bowl Cleanser

> ¼ cup borax
> ¼ cup baking soda

Pour both ingredients directly into the toilet bowl and swish with a toilet brush. Let stand at least fifteen minutes before flushing.

Commode Cleaner

> ¼ cup baking soda
> ¼ cup vinegar

Sprinkle baking soda into the bowl, followed by vinegar, and watch the reaction! Bubbles created by the chemical reaction will loosen stains. Finish the job by scrubbing with a toilet brush before flushing.

Borax the Bowl

Sprinkle ¼ cup of borax in the toilet bowl and swish with a brush before going to bed. Flush in the morning to reveal a sparkling bowl!

Be sure to keep the lid shut overnight if you have pets that might drink from the bowl.

Eco-Friendly Bowl Bleach

Pour a cup of hydrogen peroxide into the bowl and scrub with a brush. Let sit for fifteen minutes before flushing. Hydrogen peroxide works to kill germs while bleaching out hard-water stains. It works especially well on rust stains left behind from iron in the water.

Rims, Tanks, and Bases

Essential Antibacterial Spray

For this recipe, pick your favorite antibacterial essential oil, whether clove, citrus, tea tree, rosemary, thyme, or lavender. In a spray bottle, dilute 1 teaspoon of essential oil in 1 cup of water. Shake well and spray on toilet rim, back, and seat. Do not rinse.

Vinegar Spritz

For a quick deodorizer, pour some straight vinegar into a spray bottle and spray the toilet seat and rim. Do not rinse; the smell will dissipate in a few hours.

Walls

To avoid mildewy walls, wipe down with 5 drops of clove oil diluted in 2 cups of water in a spray bottle. Shake to mix before spraying on walls and wiping with a cotton cloth.

Odors

Strike a match on bathroom odors! Many chemical bathroom sprays are more offensive than the odors they are masking. Neutralize bathroom odors by striking a match. The burning sulfur smell that results literally means toilet odors have met their match! If you're looking for a longer lasting, more pleasant aroma, use the match to light an all-natural candle. Several natural candle companies produce specially formulated odor neutralizing candles, made with essential oils and other natural ingredients chosen specifically to battle tough odors. I've had the same Vermont Soy Clean Air Candle in my bathroom for years, as I only burn it for a few minutes at a time. Even though many candles are self-contained (mine is in a tin), it is important not to leave burning candles unattended.

Laundry Lessons

One of the best home investments you can make for the environment is a high-efficiency (HE) washing machine. These machines use less water and less energy while getting your clothes just as clean as standard models. Some are physically gentler on your clothes as well, so the clothes will last longer. They are also capable of spinning clothes much drier than the older agitator washing machines. This means, if you use an electric or gas clothes dryer, it will also take less energy to dry the laundry. However, like most good quality home appliances, HE washing machines are an expensive investment.

No matter what type of machine you use, you can lessen your impact on the environment by using a phosphate-free detergent without artificial scents and dyes. There are several good brands on the market, most of which also pledge not to practice animal testing. These include products made by Seventh Generation, Ecover, and Sun & Earth.

Natural laundry boosters, such as borax and washing soda, help add muscle to laundry detergents that do not use phosphates. Remember, many commercial products use phosphates because they add significant cleaning power to cleaners such as laundry and dishwasher detergents. However, phosphates are bad news for the environment, and the more people use them, the higher the toll on the world around us.

The manufacturer of 20 Mule Team borax markets its product as a water conditioner that boosts a detergent's cleaning power by "controlling alkalinity, deodorizing the clothes and aiding the removal of stains and soils." It recommends using ½ cup for regular loads along with the recommended amount of detergent, or ¾ cup for large capacity and front-loading machines.

Likewise, Arm & Hammer recommends adding ½ cup of its Super Washing Soda, along with detergent, to the beginning of a wash cycle. For large and/or heavily soiled loads a full cup is suggested. A cup of washing soda per load is also recommended as a water softener for hard-water conditions. The manufacturer cautions not to use washing soda on wool or silk fabrics.

Baking Soda Tip: If you have a hockey player in your house, be sure to give the hockey bag a good sprinkle of baking soda at the end of the season. Leave the baking soda in the bag with the pads until it is pulled out the next season, when it can be shaken out or vacuumed up. Give the inside of each glove its own shake of baking soda as well.

Baking soda is great for neutralizing smelly laundry odors, and is used in some laundry-detergent formulas. Add a cup to any load, but it is especially useful for gym clothes and sock and underwear loads.

Vinegar serves as a wonderful fabric softener, and will keep colors crisp and bright and prevent whites from graying. Just add ½ cup to the rinse cycle. If your machine has a dispenser for liquid fabric softener, pour the vinegar straight in there to the fill line.

The best trick to treating stains is to tackle them as soon as possible, before they have a chance to set. Immediate blotting with soap and water will go a long way toward getting rid of most stains. If you can't get to a stain right away, soak the garment in a sink filled with warm water, with a squirt of castile soap or a couple of Tablespoons of washing soda, until you can treat the stain. If the stain is protein based, such as blood, grass, or some food stains, use cold rather than warm water, as heat will set the stain. Cool water should also be used for fabrics that bleed their color in warmer water. Garments can be soaked for up to several hours, until you are able to wash them.

HE washing machines need a low-sudsing detergent. The following formulas can be used in either traditional machines or HE machines, but less is used in HE washers. You may never have to shop the laundry aisle again, if you follow these suggestions for natural detergent, whitener, stain remover, and starch.

The liquid laundry soap is listed first, as it works best with cold water. Using cold water to wash your laundry saves a significant amount of energy and so reduces your impact on the environment (and your water-heating budget). If you have a strong preference for laundry powder, then give powdered laundry soap a try. The simple laundry soap recipe should not be used with a cold water wash as it requires warm water to properly dissolve.

Lumpy Liquid Laundry Soap

Properly labeled, this formula can be stored in any reusable plastic jug with a tightly fitting lid, such as an old detergent or juice container. Although, it starts out a smooth liquid, it does have a tendency to get lumpy while sitting on the shelf; just be sure to give the jug a good shake before using to evenly distribute all ingredients.

Combine ½ cup of washing soda and ¼ cup of borax. Stir in 4 cups of warm water and keep stirring until all the powder is dissolved. Add ¼ cup of castile soap scented with essential oil (or unscented soap and about 10 drops of your favorite oil).

Stir to mix. Use ¼–⅓ cup per load in HE machines and ½ cup per load in standard machines.

Powdered Laundry Soap

You'll need a food processor to mix up this powdered laundry soap, as well as:

> 1 bar plain soap (without dyes or moisturizers)
> ½ cup borax
> ½ cup washing soda (or baking soda for a more delicate soap)

Grate bar of soap with the food processor's grating attachment. Switch to the chopping blade and add borax and soda to the soap. Process until the ingredients appear evenly mixed and all large peels of soap are gone. Only a couple of Tablespoons of the finished product are needed per load, and even less for HE machines. I have had some success using this formula in cold water. Using a warm-water wash cycle will ensure the soap dissolves completely.

I have an old food processor I use exclusively for making laundry soap. I do not recommend using the same processor used for cooking unless you are prepared to spend a lot of time rinsing the processor of all cleaning ingredients.

If you are fortunate enough to find a source of soap flakes, which have become increasingly sparse on the market, a cup of soap flakes can be substituted for the bar of soap in this recipe. In that case, all ingredients can be mixed by hand, and the food processor is not necessary.

Simple Laundry Soap

This formula comes out as a slightly sticky powder, but will dry to a powder if left uncovered for any length of time. I like to use a castile soap containing essential oils to add a nice scent. My favorite soap for this recipe is a liquid castile soap scented with orange oil. If using an unscented soap, you can mix in 10 drops of your favorite oil to customize your laundry soap.

Mix well 1 cup each:

> washing soda
> borax
> castile soap

Use ½ cup per load in agitator machines or ¼ cup per load in HE machines. This formula needs a warm-water wash cycle to dissolve completely. Be sure to use vinegar in the rinse cycle to combat graying that can occur with soap (rather than detergent) in hard water. If your machine has a fabric-softener dispenser, fill the dispenser with white vinegar, otherwise add ½ cup of vinegar at the beginning of the rinse cycle.

Anti-Gray Additives

Add either ¼ cup of borax or ¼ cup of vinegar to white loads to prevent graying.

Stain Pretreaters

Just Soap

A bar of plain soap, rubbed directly onto a stain, acts as a great stain remover. Be sure not to use soaps with coloring or moisturizers added, as these ingredients could add to the staining problem. Just apply the soap directly to the stain, rub the fabric together and rinse. To make the soap easier to grip, and to add a touch of scrubbing power, place the bar in the toe of an old (clean) pair of pantyhose.

For really stubborn stains, allow the soaped stain to soak in cold water a half hour before rinsing. A longer soak is okay too, as it will not harm the fabric the way many commercial pretreaters can.

Washing Soda

Arm & Hammer cautions that rubber gloves should be used when using Super Washing Soda in a solution or a paste. It recommends mixing 4 Tablespoons of washing soda in ¼ cup of warm water. Use a gloved finger to gently rub the paste onto the dampened stain, then wash as usual. Test an inconspicuous area for colorfastness before pretreating the stain.

Rust Remover

Rust stains are tough, but not insurmountable. I've had some success treating rust stains on clothes and other fabric with lemon juice and salt. Squeeze lemon juice directly onto the stain, then sprinkle on a generous amount of salt. Rub the fabric together until the stain starts to break up. Wash away the loosened rust with soap and water. Repeat the process until the stain is entirely removed.

Odor Eater

Add a cup of baking soda to the wash load to neutralize sweat and other laundry odors.

Fabric Softener

Add ½ cup of vinegar to your washer's rinse cycle to soften clothes and keep colors bright. If your washer has a special fabric-softener dispenser, pour the vinegar directly in there to the fill line.

"Dry" Cleaning

To freshen "dry clean only" items such as suit coats and heavy wool sweaters, get a large paper grocery bag. In a spray bottle, mix a couple of drops of your favorite essential oil diluted in a cup of water and shake well. Lightly spray the inside of the bag with this solution. (The spray isn't strictly necessary, but does help combat odors in the clothes.) Add 1 cup of wheat bran in the bottom of the bag and place the garment in the bag. Roll down the top of the bag and shake for five minutes or until your arms get really tired, whichever comes first. Open the bag and shake the bran off the garment, back into the bottom of the bag. Brush with a lint brush and you're ready to go!

Simple Starches

First Starch

In a spray bottle mix:

> 1 Tablespoon cornstarch
> 2 cups cold water

Shake the bottle to dissolve the cornstarch and spray onto fabric as you would commercial spray starch. This method is best for whites, and not recommended for dark fabrics.

Second Starch

Another way to make starch is to add extra water when cooking rice. To make a cup of spray starch, add an extra ½ cup of water to plain rice then pour it off a few minutes prior to the end of the cooking time. Dilute the starchy water in a spray bottle with ½ cup of plain cold water.

Living Areas

Here are some maintenance tips for those "public" parts of the home, including family rooms, living rooms, dens, offices, and dining rooms.

Dusting and Vacuuming

The vacuum is my most relied upon cleaning tool. I use it in every room of the house, from ceiling to floor. Notice I did not say from floor to ceiling, and for good reason. I always clean a room from the top down. That way dust wiped from a tabletop won't have a chance to relocate on a freshly cleaned floor.

I have a dust allergy, and can't tolerate dusters that sweep the dust back into the air. To avoid this I use two tools: my vacuum and microfiber dusting cloths. The first step involves putting the upholstery brush attachment at the end of the long extension arm, in order to reach the ceiling. Brush the cobwebs and dust from the ceiling, paying special attention to crevices and corners. Unlike the hard-plastic corner attachment, the brush will not leave marks or scratches on the ceiling and walls. Continue on down the corners of the walls and over window casings, curtains, pictures, paintings, and other wall decorations.

If the brush attachment becomes dirty or clogged, simply remove it from the vacuum hose and run the hose nozzle over the brush. Once the walls and ceiling are dusted, remove the extension arm and apply the brush directly to the end of the vacuum hose. The next step is to tackle the furniture, again from the top down. For instance, start with the shade of a tabletop lamp before moving down to the base of the lamp and other large objects on the table. Then vacuum the tabletop, sides, underneath the top, and the legs. Don't forget to remove small objects that could be sucked up by the vacuum. These will need to be hand-dusted. The final step is to go over everything with a microfiber dusting cloth to gather any dust the vacuum may have missed.

Vacuuming Tip: *If you have an area with a lot of small objects, try using a rubber band to secure a cotton-weave rag, such as part of an old T-shirt, directly over the vacuum hose nozzle. This idea came to me when I needed a way to clean my "indoor beach." I kept a shallow planter box on the floor of my music room in front of a large set of windows. I filled the bottom of the box with beach sand and seashells, and placed potted plants atop the sand. I loved the little beach, but dreaded cleaning it. I was constantly picking out fallen leaves, dead flowers, and cluster-fly carcasses. I couldn't vacuum these out without sucking up a significant amount of sand, until I cut a square from an old T-shirt and held it over the nozzle. I brought a trashcan next to the planter, and would turn the vacuum off over the can and the dirt and unwanted objects would fall into the trash. I soon discovered this technique also worked well for general dusting of knickknacks.*

Of course the upholstery brush is also perfect for vacuuming couches, chairs, and other upholstered furniture. I also use it on baseboards to avoid scratches and marks that the corner attachment might make. Once I've worked my way down to floor level I switch to the corner nozzle and work my way around the edges of the room. Finally, I'm ready to vacuum the floor.

If your vacuum gives you a choice of heads, only use the beater head on carpets. The beater brush will scatter dust on a hard surface floor and it has a tendency to suck up small area rugs.

Carpet/Fabric Stains

There's more than one way to break up and remove a stain; the best way depends upon what caused the mess. Soap and water are among the best ways to treat a stain, but water temperature plays a critical role. Protein-based stains need to be treated with cold, as heat will set the stain. This includes stains caused by substances such as blood, grass, and some foods such as eggs. Fat-based stains, left by oily substances, are better removed with soap and hot water, which helps to break up the stain. If you're not sure what type of stain you're dealing with—or if it's something like spaghetti sauce that has both fats and protein—be sure to treat first with cold. If a cold treatment alone does not take up all the stain, then treat with warm water and soap. With either application, only use enough water to work the suds up into a lather; too much water can cause the stain to spread.

If it's just plain dirt you're dealing with, it generally takes an abrasive material to loosen the spot and an absorbent material to lift it. One thing to keep in mind when cleaning rugs, carpet, and upholstery is to use the minimum amount of liquid necessary to get the job done. You don't want the stain to spread and you don't want to be left with a wet spot on your favorite chair that takes days to dry! Here are a variety of techniques to try when dealing with stains on carpets, rugs, and upholstered furniture:

Baking-Soda Solution

Sprinkle baking soda on the mark and rub, from the outside to the center, with a sponge dampened with vinegar. Rinse the sponge and wring it out thoroughly, then use it to wipe up the baking soda and the dirt. Here, the baking soda acts as a mild abrasive and will also neutralize any odor from the mess. When dry, vacuum up any remaining baking soda.

A Bran-New Way

Wheat bran is both abrasive and absorbent. Activate it as a spot cleaner with a small amount of vinegar. First, sprinkle bran over the dirty spot, then mist with vinegar in a spray bottle. Rub the area with a clean rag or kitchen towel. The moistened bran will start to clump together as you rub. Collect the bran in the towel to discard, then vacuum the area. If the stain is on a particularly delicate fabric, test an inconspicuous spot first.

Club-Soda Stain Clobberer

Clobber fresh stains with club soda. Simply pour on a small amount, rub, and wipe the stain away. This works best for fresh food stains on upholstery, but has also proven successful on rugs and carpets.

Fresh-Stain Fighter

Cornstarch will absorb fresh liquid stains. Sprinkle enough to fully cover the stain and vacuum after about five minutes.

Pet-Accident Rescue

After removing solids, dab on a solution of ¾ cup of club soda and ¼ cup of vinegar. Blot until clean, reapplying as necessary.

The All-Around Cure

Some stains require a little bit of everything to get the job done. Among those particularly nasty stains are vomit and pet feces. These stains often contain fats and proteins, as well as a foul odor. Start by picking up and discarding as much of the solid material as possible. I use toilet paper and dump the solids in the toilet to be flushed away. Use paper towels or a washable rag to blot up any liquid, then cover

the stain with baking soda. The baking soda will help absorb liquid as well as neutralize odor. Rub the spot with vinegar on a sponge and leave the spot to dry. Vacuum once the area is dry. If there is still staining, mix castile soap with a small amount of cold water and apply to the stain with a scrub brush. Repeat with soap and warm water. Dab with a damp sponge to rinse. If any odor remains, reapply baking soda and vacuum once dry.

Carpet Deodorizers

Sometimes a carpet needs more than a vacuuming but less than a scrubbing. Instead of sprinkling an artificial, flowery, commercial deodorizer on your rug or carpet, try absorbing the bad odors with 100 percent baking soda. Let the baking soda sit for several hours or overnight before vacuuming.

In a hurry? For a quicker fix, mix two parts cornmeal and one part borax together and sprinkle over the carpet. This mix will absorb carpet odors in about an hour, then vacuum as usual.

Walls

Scrub tough wall stains, such as greasy fingerprints or crayon marks, with baking soda on a damp sponge. Rinse with a clean sponge.

Leather Furniture Cleaner

Lemon juice is an excellent leather cleaner, be it applied with a cloth or straight from a halved lemon.

Leather, like wood, benefits from an occasional oiling. Nourish your leather by rubbing with a cloth that's saturated with olive oil and a drop or two of lemon, orange, or grapefruit essential oil. It's convenient to premix these ingredients in a jar with a tightly fitting lid. Shake vigorously to mix and dip your cloth in the jar to apply. Rub the oil into the leather, then buff with a separate, dry cloth. Allow the oil to sink into the leather before using the furniture. To avoid oil stains on clothing, test for saturation by pressing a thin, light-colored cloth (such as a cloth diaper) onto the furniture. Do not use the furniture unless the cloth comes up clean and the leather no longer feels greasy to the touch. This shouldn't be a problem if you buff thoroughly.

Slate and Marble Floors

Wash these and other natural stone materials with a solution of 1 cup of baking soda and 1 cup of lemon juice added to a bucket of water. Rinse thoroughly and buff dry with a cotton towel.

Finished Wood Floors

There are many options for cleaning sealed wood floors, not the least of which is a capful of castile soap in a bucket of water. As with any hard floor, it's best to vacuum before mopping or scrubbing. Avoid sweeping, if possible, as it scatters small dust particles into the air. I almost never sweep indoor surfaces with a broom. Instead I use a vacuum or nonelectric sweeper.

Tea Treatment

Want to get one more use out of an old tea bag? Tea leaves were once a popular way to polish wood floors. I like to make batches of sun tea. When the tea is brewed, I throw the used bags (four to six of them) into a bucket of warm water and use it to mop my pine floors. Just be sure your tea bags contain only real tea leaves, and not herbs or flowers that could stain your floor.

"Salad Dressing" Wood-Floor Polish

Wood floors, like wood furniture, benefit from the occasional application of oil. Oil helps to restore and retain moisture in the wood, maintaining the wood's natural luster and preventing cracking. A good floor polish should accomplish this, in addition to cleaning away dirt. Mixing oil and vinegar accomplishes both tasks—it's not just for salads anymore!

Combine equal parts olive oil and white vinegar in a spray bottle. Shake well and apply to the bottom of a dust mop. The dust mop will pick up any dirt and dust the vacuum left behind while polishing the wood. Be sure to periodically shake the mop outdoors, and reapply the polish to keep from simply redistributing the dirt to another part of your floor.

If you don't have a dust mop, the job can also be accomplished on your hands and knees with a cotton towel.

Feel free to experiment with your oils. If you don't like the scent of olive oil, try using almond, walnut, or even plain vegetable cooking oil. You can also dress up the scent by adding a dozen drops of your favorite essential oil to the spray bottle.

Unfinished Wood Floors

For unfinished floors, it's best to mop with vinegar and water. For really dirty unfinished floors, sprinkle the surface with baking soda and scrub with a brush dipped in a diluted vinegar solution (a couple of cups of vinegar in a bucket of water). Rinse with a mop and plain water.

Furniture Polish

Polish and nourish wood furniture with pure almond or walnut oil. Wipe the oil on with a clean cotton rag. Follow up by buffing with a dry cotton cloth or towel. A few drops of vanilla extract added to the oil leaves behind a warm and welcoming scent.

Wood Cleaner

Olive oil is another good choice for polishing wood furniture, and more readily available than almond oil and walnut oil. Mix 2 parts olive oil to 1 part vinegar or lemon juice to boost the cleaning power. This formula can be made in a spray bottle; shake to mix before each use. For even distribution, it's best to spray the polish onto your cleaning cloth rather than directly on furniture.

For a faster-drying polish/cleanser, mix ½ cup of lemon juice with ¼ cup of vinegar and ¼ cup of food-grade linseed oil. Apply and polish with a lint-free cotton cloth.

Painless Window Washing

Why is it that so many of us dread washing windows? Perhaps it's because it is not a job you can do halfheartedly. A window streaked with cleaning fluid looks just as bad as, and often worse than, the dirty window you started with. In addition, many of us have been raised to believe nothing short of half a roll of paper towels is needed to do the job properly. It just seems like such a waste. Then there is the smell of ammonia or the perfumed surfactants that are key ingredients in many commercial cleansers.

The good news is that there is a better way. In fact, there are several better ways. Paper towels can be replaced by a slew of other tools that are either reusable or, in the case of newspaper, a new use for a used-up product. What's more, those smelly and often toxic cleaners are not needed—not even on the dirtiest windows. This section contains formulas and techniques for cleaning windows, mirrors, and other glass products. Give them each a try and see what works best for you. You're sure to find there's more than one way to clean a window.

Window Washing Tip: When washing windows inside and out, use vertical strokes on one side and horizontal strokes on the other. That way, if you are left with streaks you know which side to touch up.

Abrasives

If you have something hard, gooey, or sticky that just won't come off with regular glass-cleaning techniques you may need to scrape it off. This can be done with the careful use of a razor blade or by scrubbing with an abrasive substance. I recommend salt as a mild abrasive that is less likely to scratch the surface of the glass. Then clean the rest of the glass as usual.

Newspaper

As they say, it's all right there in black and white. Perhaps the simplest way to clean a window is to wad up a piece of dry newspaper and rub it on the glass. Rather than dirtying glass, the ink leaves windows and mirrors shining. While dry newspaper isn't the best choice for windows stained with fly spots or dog-nose smudges, it works just fine for your run-of-the mill dust and fingerprints. Use newspaper with the vinegar-and-water spray below for those tougher marks and smudges.

Squeegee

Like newspaper, a squeegee is a tool that can be used with any of the spray-on glass-cleaner recipes below. Professional window washers use squeegees for a streak-free shine, no doubt saving reams of paper and countless trees. A short-handled squeegee is a handy tool to have around the house. In addition to windows, a squeegee can be used to remove excess water from shower walls and doors—performing the same function as the post-shower surfactant sprays that are sold by many chemical cleaning-product manufacturers.

Diluted Vinegar Spray

A very effective glass cleaner can be made by diluting ¼ to ½ cup of vinegar with 2 cups of water. Mix the two together in a reusable spray bottle and you're good to go. However, if you have been using commercial glass cleaners, it is likely they have left behind a surfactant film that will cause diluted vinegar to leave streaks. If this is the case, just add a few drops of liquid soap to the mix to break down the film. After a cleaning or two, you can leave out the soap.

Cornstarch Glass Cleaner

This is my favorite way to clean glass. It is a diluted version of the formula known as "ooblick," a favorite tactile pastime of many preschoolers.

Mix warm water and cornstarch in a bowl in approximately a 2 to 1 ratio; ¼ cup of cornstarch and ½ cup of water should be enough to do most jobs. Apply to the glass using a cotton cloth such as a dish towel, old T-shirt, or clean rag (just be sure the rag won't leave lint behind). Keep rubbing with the cloth until the film disappears. Switch to a dry part of the cloth and polish to a brilliant shine.

So there you have it, cleaning windows really can be fun! What's more, you won't believe the results.

Air Freshening and Scents

Commercial air fresheners make my allergies go wild. I prefer to freshen the air with more subtle herbs and essential oils that don't assault my senses.

Potpourri

In the summer I gather flowers, mints, and other fragrant herbs from my gardens to dry into custom potpourri. When it's fresh I display the potpourri in tea saucers and shallow bowls throughout the house, and especially in the bathrooms. In the dead of winter, when the potpourri's potency has waned, I reuse it by tossing a couple of Tablespoons full into the water container atop my woodstove. To refresh old potpourri, drizzle on one of the oil blends listed at the end of this section.

Flowers and herbs are easily dried by hanging them upside down, in small bunches, after picking. To speed the drying process, remove unwanted stems and leaves and place them in a single layer on a cookie sheet. Bake in a 250°F (120°C) oven for several hours, until dry and crispy.

Essential Oils

Essential oils can be diffused into the air by several methods, including the woodstove method described above for potpourri. There are also special lightbulb rings on the market that hold oils and diffuse them through the heat of a conventional lightbulb. Note that these rings do not work with energy-efficient compact fluorescent bulbs. Not only do the rings not fit on most compact fluorescents, these bulbs conserve energy by producing more light and less heat.

You can disperse your favorite oil without heat by mixing several drops in a spray bottle of water. Shake well before spraying into the air or on absorbent surfaces, such as floor coverings, that can harbor unwanted odors.

Candles

I love to burn candles, but I'm very picky about what type I light in my house. I'm loyal to all-natural candles scented only with essential oils, with no dyes or chemical additives. Look for brands that pledge to use natural waxes such as soy or beeswax. Wicks should also be made from a natural material, such as unbleached cotton or hemp. Avoid candles with lead wick bases, which can emit toxic fumes if the candle burns too low. Two good brands I use are Way Out Wax and Vermont Naturals. Way Out Wax's Clean Air candle contains an odor-neutralizing blend of essential oils.

Common sense should always be applied in using candles. In addition to making sure candles are secure in an area out of reach of little hands and away from flammables, special attention should be paid to any smoke emitted. Candles giving off white or black smoke or soot are polluting the air. Breathing such smoke is equivalent to breathing in diesel exhaust. Always trim long wicks to less than ¼ inch before lighting, and pay special attention when extinguishing candles to be sure they go all the way out—never let a candle smolder.

Clean Air Room Spray

Clean Air room spray is a natural spray made from the same proprietary blend as the Clean Air candles, marketed by Way Out Wax. This spray is an all-natural alternative to chemical air-freshener sprays and does not uses a CFC propellant, so it is safe for the ozone layer as well as your home. Way Out Wax founder and president Jim Rossiter reports that this blend is even used in the industrial waste-hauling industry to neutralize odors around commercial dumpsters located in densely populated areas.

Diffusers

Reed oil diffusers are all the rage these days. These are glass jars or pottery filled with essential-oil mixtures or other scented elixirs. Dried reeds, about twice the length of the jar height, are placed in the liquid. Because reeds are porous, the liquid easily penetrates the stems. The tiny holes in the stem draw the liquid upward like a straw. When the liquid reaches the top, it evaporates into the air.

If you have a reed diffuser that has spent all its liquid, you can reuse the jar and reeds. Create your own scent using your favorite essential oil or a combination of oils. For ideas, read the descriptions of your favor-

ite scented candles, or use one of the oil combinations listed below. Because essential oils are both potent and expensive, the recipes in this book are mixed with carrier oils, such as almond oil. Carrier oils soften the scent of the essential oils, and soften the impact on your wallet.

To make a diffuser from scratch you'll need to start with a pretty jar, bottle, or bud vase. Make sure the container you choose is water-tight. The neck of the container should be wide enough to hold the reeds, but not much wider. This will allow the reeds to stand erect and reduce the chance of the oil getting dusty or spilling out if jostled. If you can't locate reeds, look around your garden, the woods, or a local swamp for hollow-stemmed plant stalks that you can dry. Dried cat-tails, bamboo, hydrangea, or daylily stems will do the trick. Each lends a different look to the final product, so try and pick a container and diffuser stems that complement each other.

Get creative by mixing up a scent you think matches the look you've created. For example, use a more substantial stock, such as a cattail, in a rustic brown or green jar. Match the scent by using earthy essential oils such as cedar, spruce, and patchouli. Or create a light and airy arrangement with dried hydrangea stems in a cobalt blue vase containing fresh scents such as eucalyptus or lemon oil.

Making Scents

Essential-oil blends can be used in many ways to freshen the air around your home. The following blends can be used in reed diffusers, lightbulb rings, dripped in a pot of water on the woodstove, or drizzled onto a collection of pretty stones, seashells, or sea glass contained in an odd teacup or saucer. Oil blends can also be used to recharge potpourri that has lost its potency.

The easiest blend to make is simply diluting your favorite essential oil in a milder, less-expensive carrier oil, such as almond oil, or even the olive oil or sesame oil you use for cooking.

To make an air-freshener spray, replace the carrier oil with water. These spritzers are fun and easy to mix in 16-ounce plastic spray bottles, set to the finest mist spray. Shake well before each use.

By cutting down the recipes they can also be mixed for smaller containers, such as perfume diffusers. Tap water works fine, unless your water has a strong smell from minerals such as sulfur or treatment chemicals such as chlorine. In that case, I recommend buying a jug of distilled water to use when mixing up spritzers.

> **Air Freshener Tip:** *People in the business of making naturally scented products will tell you their top seller, hands down, is lavender. So if you're entertaining, or otherwise looking for something to please a crowd, lavender or a lavender blend is a good way to go.*

Lavender Rosemary

Mix 8 to 10 drops each of lavender and rosemary essential oils with ¼ cup of olive oil in a jar with a tightly fitting lid. Shake to blend.

Rosemary Mint

Mix 5 drops of rosemary and 7 drops of spearmint oils with ¼ cup of almond oil in a jar with a tightly fitting lid. Shake to blend.

Toasty Citrus

Mix 10 drops of orange oil and 5 drops of lemon oil with ¼ cup of sesame oil in a jar with a tightly fitting lid. Shake to blend.

Favorite Forest

Mix 5 drops each of pine, spruce, and cedar oils with ¼ cup of sesame oil in a jar with a tightly fitting lid. Shake to blend.

Bedrooms

Many of the cleaning techniques previously outlined for living areas also apply to bedrooms. However, whether your bedroom serves as a haven from a hectic household or just a place to sleep, here are some tips to keeping it clean and inviting.

Clothes Storage

Keep your clothes fresh by introducing scents to your drawers and closets. Cedar is a popular way to deter pests such as moths and mice from getting into long-term clothes-storage areas. But you don't need an expensive cedar-lined chest to reap the benefits cedar has to offer. Cedar shavings are often sold in small sachet-style bags that are easy to tuck anywhere—from drawers to under-the-bed storage bins. Likewise, blocks of cedar are sold for this purpose.

It's easy to make your own sachet filled with cedar shavings, your favorite potpourri, or simply dried flowers. Sew a handful of your chosen filling (I'm partial to dried lavender flowers and rose petals) into a folded-over piece of muslin or cheesecloth. To reinfuse an old sachet with new life, just dab the outside with a few drops of essential oil.

Cedar Tip: If you have cedar blocks in drawers, closets, chests, or other storage containers that aren't giving off much scent any more, rub them a bit with sandpaper. This exposes new wood to the air, and your blocks can get back to work keeping your clothes smelling nice and safe from pests.

Bed Linens

Dust mites, and what they leave behind, are the major cause of most dust allergies. Keep dust mites at bay by sealing your mattresses and pillows inside covers especially designed to keep out mites. Follow the manufacturer's instructions for laundering.

Mattress Odors

Neutralize urine and sweat odors by lightly dampening the spot with a fine spray of water or a spritzer as described in the "Making Scents" section above. Sprinkle borax on the mattress, rubbing problem areas. Once dry, vacuum clean.

Part 3

THE TOP TEN RECIPES

This, the "cookbook" section, is designed to serve as a quick reference guide to my top ten favorite make-ahead formulas. These are my cleaning-pantry staples and my first line of defense against a dirty house. In conjunction with the make-as-you-use formulas previously outlined, these recipes can replace virtually every commercial cleaning product you currently have in your home. The main exception is automatic dishwasher detergent. I have yet to find a quality formula to take on that task. There is an "emergency" recipe listed in the kitchen section of the guide, but it tends to leave a white film on glassware and I do not recommend it for regular use. Included here is, however, a lovely dish soap designed for hand washing.

Also not listed in this section are recipes for laundry products. Formulas for laundry products are listed in the laundry section of this guide.

Whereas part 2 outlined general recipes and techniques for various cleaning jobs, the formulas that follow are those that I have customized and refined to be my favorite "products." They are variations on themes described earlier, but these specific recipes are not detailed elsewhere in this guide.

The recipes that follow are listed alphabetically by the job they do.

1. Air Freshener

Lavender-Vanilla Mist

In a 16-ounce spray bottle mix:

> 10 drops lavender oil
> 5 drops vanilla extract
> 15 ounces distilled water or quality well or spring water

Set bottle to the finest mist setting. Shake prior to each use.

2. All-Purpose Kitchen Spray

Kitchen Keeper

In a 32-ounce spray bottle mix in the given order:

> 1 Tablespoon castile soap with an essential oil, such as pep-permint, orange, or lavender
> OR 1 Tablespoon unscented castile soap and 8–10 drops of your favorite essential oil
> 3 cups water
> 1 cup vinegar
> 1 Tablespoon lemon juice

Shake to mix before each use.

3. Appliance Cleaner

Grime-Away Spray

In a 32-ounce spray bottle mix in the given order:

> 1 teaspoon castile soap with an essential oil
> OR 1 teaspoon unscented castile soap and 8–10 drops of your
>   favorite oil
> 1 teaspoon washing soda
> 3 cups warm water
> 1 Tablespoon vinegar

Shake well to mix before each use.

4. Bathroom Spray

Minty-Clean Spray

In a 16-ounce or larger spray bottle mix in the given order:

> 1 Tablespoon peppermint castile soap
> 1 cup warm water
> ¼ teaspoon tea tree oil
> 12 drops spearmint oil
> ½ cup vinegar

Shake to mix before each use.

5. Dish Soap

Rosemary-Mint Wash

In a squeeze bottle or pump soap dispenser combine:

> 8 ounces peppermint or unscented castile soap
> 10 drops spearmint oil
> 10 drops rosemary oil

Not only does this formula smell great on your hands, the rosemary and spearmint essential oils add an antibacterial boost to the wash.

6. Disinfecting Spray

Dandy Disinfectant

In a 16-ounce or larger spray bottle mix in the given order:

> 1 teaspoon borax
> 1 cup water
> ½ cup vinegar
> ¼ teaspoon tea tree oil
> 5 drops spearmint oil
> 5 drops lavender oil
> 5 drops rosemary oil

Shake well prior to use.

7. Furniture Polish

Citrus Polish

In a spray bottle combine:

> ½ cup olive oil
> ¼ cup lemon juice
> 5 drops orange essential oil

Shake well and apply small amount to cotton cloth.

8. Glass Cleaner

Streak-Free Shiner

In a 16-ounce or larger spray bottle mix in the given order:

> ¼ teaspoon castile soap
> 1²/₃ cups water
> ¼ cup vinegar

Shake well before use. After spraying, wipe the glass with newspaper, a squeegee, or a lint-free cotton cloth. A little of this mixture goes a long way, and it can be stored for future use.

9. Scouring Powder

Mold-Attack Scouring Powder

In a container with a shaker top combine:

> ²/₃ cup baking soda
> ¹/₃ cup borax

Stir ingredients to combine then put on shaker lid, or place a piece of plastic wrap under the secured lid and shake to mix.

Dampen moldy areas with a sponge, if needed. (It's likely the area is already damp, hence the mold.) Shake on powder and let sit a few minutes before wiping away. Rinse well.

10. Wood Floor Polish

Vanilla-Almond Floor Shine

Mix in a 16-ounce or larger spray bottle:

> 1 cup almond oil
> ½ cup vinegar
> 10 drops vanilla extract

Shake vigorously and spray onto the bottom of a dust mop. Reapply as needed.

RESOURCES

Association of Vermont Recyclers. "Homemade Household Cleaners RecipeBook."www.vtrecyclers.org/files/HH%20RECIPES%20Booklet%20for%20web.pdf

Clean Calgary Association. "Green Cleaning Guide." www.cleancalgary.org/images/uploads/File/GreenCleaning.pdf

Annie Berthold-Bond. *Clean & Green*. Woodstock, NY: Ceres Press, 1994.

Karyn Siegel-Maier. *The Naturally Clean Home*. North Adams, MA: Storey Publishing, 1999.

Shannon Lush and Jennifer Fleming. *Spotless: Room-by-Room Solutions to Domestic Disasters*. London: Ebury Press, 2008.

Editors of FC&A Publishing. *Fast Fixes & Simple Solutions: Surprising Uses for Ordinary Household Items.* Peachtree, GA: FC&A Publishing, 2002.

20 Mule Team. "Borax Laundry Booster: A Guide to Laundry and Household Uses." www.purex.com/documents/borax.pdf

Arm & Hammer. "Super Washing Soda Usage Tips." www.thelaundry-basket.com/Usage_Tips/Usage_Tips_Super_Washing_Soda/usage_tips_super_washing_soda.html

Seventh Generation. Cleaning products and information at www
.seventhgeneration.com.

Way Out Wax. Candles and clean air products at www.wayoutwax
.com.

ACKNOWLEDGMENTS

Many thanks to all who helped compile the traditional know-how in these pages. Truly, what was old is new again as we return to a simpler, less chemically driven way of life. Thanks to Jim Rossiter of Way Out Wax, who is always willing to share his resources and expertise in the realm of essential oils, natural ingredients, and life in general. Thanks to the online community members who shared their grandmother's secrets, their personal tips, and directed me to other sources of information. Thanks to my "real life" friends and family who provided assistance and encouragement along the way, especially my dad who also lent his scientific expertise and keen editor's eye. My sincere gratitude goes out to Morrisville, Vermont, retailers Apple Tree Natural Foods, Price Chopper Supermarket, and Country Home Center for their cooperation in allowing me to photograph products. I am also most grateful to the Chelsea Green team who gave me the opportunity to publish this guide, and worked with me to shape the final product. Special thanks to my husband, Dan, and children, Adriana and Ian, who supported me emotionally throughout this entire process and didn't laugh at my crazy experiments.

THE CHELSEA GREEN GUIDES

Chelsea Green's new *Green Guides* are perfect tutors for individuals or businesses looking to green-up their knowledge. Each compact, value-priced guide is packed with tips that will improve the environment and your finances.

SUSTAINABLE FOOD:
How to Buy Right and Spend Less
ELISE MCDONOUGH
9781603581417
$7.95

CLIMATE CHANGE:
Simple Things You Can Do
to Make a Difference
JON CLIFT and AMANDA CUTHBERT
9781603581066
$7.95

ENERGY:
Use Less—Save More
JON CLIFT and AMANDA CUTHBERT
9781933392721
$7.95

WATER:
Use Less—Save More
JON CLIFT and AMANDA CUTHBERT
9781933392738
$7.95

Slim enough to fit in a kitchen or desk drawer, you'll return to the *Green Guides* frequently for concise, sage advice.

GREENING YOUR OFFICE
JON CLIFT and AMANDA CUTHBERT
9781933392998
$7.95

BIKING TO WORK
RORY MCMULLAN
9781933392981
$7.95

COMPOSTING:
An Easy Household Guide
NICKY SCOTT
9781933392745
$7.95

REDUCE, REUSE, RECYCLE:
An Easy Household Guide
NICKY SCOTT
9781933392752
$7.95